# YOUR
# NEW
# POTTY

# YOUR NEW POTTY

## JOANNA COLE

PHOTOGRAPHS BY

MARGARET MILLER

MORROW JUNIOR BOOKS / NEW YORK

Printed in Singapore.
1  2  3  4  5  6  7  8  9  10

Library of Congress Cataloging-in-Publication Data
Cole, Joanna.
Your new potty / by Joanna Cole ; photographs by Margaret Miller.
p.     cm.
Summary: Steffie and Ben learn how to use the potty as they make the transition from diapers to underpants.
ISBN 0-688-06105-2. ISBN 0-688-06106-0 (lib. bdg.). ISBN 0-688-08966-6 (pbk.)
1. Toilet training—Juvenile literature. [1. Toilet training.]
I. Miller, Margaret, ill. II. Title.
HQ770.5.C65 1989
649′.62—dc19     88-39862     CIP     AC

# YOUR
# NEW
# POTTY

# A Note to Parents

"Everyone tells me to relax about teaching my toddler to use the potty," said a mother recently. "It would be a lot easier to relax if I just knew what I was doing!"

These words express the feelings of many parents. Mothers and fathers are not born knowing how to help a child learn to use the toilet. They need practical information about what to do and what to expect, but in the past, advice was often misguided, and sometimes actually harmful. Fortunately, researchers have learned a great deal in recent years about toddlers and their development, and this new knowledge is now available to parents. It can make your child's transition from diapers to underpants a lot smoother.

**Patience, Not Pressure**
Before beginning, the most important thing to know is that there is no place for pressure, punishment, scolding, or shaming in teaching a child to use the toilet. The process can be compared to teaching a child to ride a two-wheel bike. Few parents would scold or punish her for tipping over. In

toileting as well, negatives only work against the learning process. Parents can help best through patient guidance and encouragement.

**Not Too Early**

The second most important rule is "Don't rush into things." Studies show that, whether teaching starts early or late, the average age when toddlers learn to use the toilet for daytime urine and BMs is twenty-eight months. This means that a child who was started at eighteen months and one who was started at twenty-six months may well end up using the toilet at the same age.

It's important to note that twenty-eight months is just an *average* age. Every child is an individual who develops at his or her own speed, and being early or late is not a reflection of a child's future abilities. Many perfectly normal, intelligent children are late-bloomers and may not be ready until age three or after.

**Is Your Child Ready?**

To get a sense of when your child is ready for toileting, you can watch for physical, mental, and emotional signs.

PHYSICAL READINESS: In babies and toddlers, physical control over the bladder and bowel develops gradually. Most children achieve bowel control before bladder control, but there is a great deal of variation.

Watch for these signs that indicate readiness in your toddler: regularity in bowel movements; pausing in play while having a BM; and staying dry for an hour or two during the day.

MENTAL READINESS: In addition to physical readiness, toddlers must be ready mentally as well. They need to understand that the products of elimination come from their own bodies. To a baby or young toddler, this basic biological fact may not be so obvious. To him, urine and feces may seem to "appear" magically in the diaper from time to time. So if your toddler tells you that he is having or has had a bowel movement, welcome this announcement with enthusiasm. Even though it may be too late to use the potty, his self-awareness is a sign that he is moving toward readiness.

EMOTIONAL READINESS: Children also must mature emotionally before they are ready for toileting. Signs of emotional readiness include wanting to be grown-up, imitating adults and older children, wanting to be clean and neat, and asking to have a diaper changed.

Not all children show all of these readiness signs, but most will show some of them between the ages of two and three. When you notice a few signs, you can take advantage of them by gradually preparing your toddler for toileting.

## Preparing Your Toddler

Even though your young toddler may not be ready to use the potty all, or even some, of the time, she will still benefit from a relaxed period of preparation—a time when she can get used to the idea of toileting with *no* pressure to perform. You will probably want to begin this preparation sometime between the ages of eighteen and twenty-six months, depending on your child's readiness. Here's how:

HELP YOUR CHILD RECOGNIZE HIS BODY SIGNALS: In preparing for toileting, teach your child to recognize that urine and feces come from his or her own body. If you see your toddler having a bowel movement, you can say, "Emily is having a BM." If your child urinates without a diaper, mention it. If she tells you she has had or is having a BM, praise her. In time, she will begin telling you *before* the movement.

SHOW YOUR TODDLER WHAT TO DO: Allow your child to observe adults or older children using the toilet or potty to show him what is expected of him. Reading him a children's potty book like this one also teaches him what toileting is all about.

GET A POTTY: Buy or borrow a potty and let your toddler take her time getting used to it. Have her try it with clothes on at first. Later, if she's reluctant to sit on the potty without a diaper because it feels a little cold, explain that it will warm up quickly.

COMMUNICATE YOUR EXPECTATIONS: Let your child know that you are confident that when she has grown up a little, she will learn to use the toilet all the time, just like the adults she knows.

ENCOURAGE POTTY PRACTICE: Ask your child to sit on the potty and "have a little try." If he does urinate or have a BM, praise him and give him a hug. Also praise him if he asks to have his diaper removed so he can use the potty.

In warm surroundings, leave the diaper off for an hour or two with the potty nearby, and mention that he can use it if he has to.

During this preparation period, there is no need to demand performance. It is enough for a toddler to find out how his body works and to learn what the potty is for. The preparation period has no time limit. It may last for a few weeks or for many months—as long as is necessary for your particular child.

## The Switch to Underpants

When your toddler has shown signs of readiness, *and* has had plenty of time for potty practice, it may be time to give up diapers for underpants in the daytime. Most toddlers will be ready for this transition sometime between the ages of two and three, but if your child has not asked to give up the diaper and/or shown definite signs of readiness, don't push it.

For the first few days or weeks, your child will probably have quite a few accidents while wearing the pants. This is perfectly normal, and in fact, accidents are helpful: They help him learn that underpants don't work the way diapers do.

The best way to handle accidents is to reassure your child, clean up calmly, and remind him to use the potty next time. Accidents will dwindle in number as time goes on.

**To Flush or Not to Flush?**
If your toddler enjoys flushing, that's fine. But some children are nervous about it. To a toddler, the productions of his body may seem like a precious part of himself, and he may be frightened to see them going down the toilet.

If your child is sensitive about flushing, wait until he is busy with something else before pouring the contents of the potty into the toilet and flushing them away—especially when he is first learning. Over time, you can help him gain control of his fears by allowing him to do the pouring and flushing himself. Often, waving good-bye to the feces and learning where they go (to the sewer system or septic tank) are reassuring to some children.

**Giving Up the Nighttime Diaper**
At naptime and bedtime, your toddler will probably still need a diaper for a while. Watch for dry nights, and when your child seems ready, experiment with leaving the diaper off.

Some children take longer than others to achieve dryness at night, and experts say that under the age of six, there is no cause for worry if your child still wets the bed. If you are concerned about this, your pediatrician may be able to help.

**Setbacks Are Normal**
It is common for children who have learned to use the potty to have periods when they begin to wet and even to soil again. Usually such regres-

sions are related to stress caused by a change in the child's normal routine. Getting a new sibling, losing a regular baby-sitter, moving to a new house, going away on vacation, starting nursery school, even catching a cold—all these can cause regression in a toddler. Usually these lapses last for only a few days to a week. The best way to handle them is to remain calm and reassuring—and wait them out.

**How to Use This Book**
Reading this book with your child can be a good part of his general preparation for toileting. By listening to the story about Steffie and Ben and their adventures with the potty, children learn exactly what parents expect of them.

In the story, you'll notice that the two children seem to learn the same skills at the same time, but this is for literary convenience only. It is not what to expect from your toddler and her friends. In real life, each child develops independently according to his or her own schedule.

Neither should you expect instant results from reading this book. It would be a rare toddler who learned to use the potty directly after listening to the book. Instead, most children will be interested in hearing the story and looking at the pictures occasionally over time. Even after giving up diapers, some children may still want to read a potty book. Perhaps this is a way of reminding themselves how much they have grown up.

**For More Information . . .**
If questions come up as your child is learning to use the toilet, your pediatrician is your best source of guidance and advice. In addition, you may find answers in *Parents*™ *Book of Toilet Teaching* (available in paperback from Ballantine Books), or in other books recommended by your librarian or bookseller.

When you were a baby, Mommy and Daddy took care of you. They fed you. They dressed you. They carried you everywhere.

When you were a baby, you cried if your
diaper was wet or messy.

14

Mommy or Daddy changed you. Then
you were clean and dry and happy again.

Now you can do a lot of things all by yourself. You can eat by yourself. You can get dressed by yourself. You can walk and run.

And you can talk, too. Now you can tell
Mommy or Daddy when your diaper
needs changing.

Mommy and Daddy are so proud of you!

Steffie is a little girl just your age. She wears diapers, too.

Steffie lives in a house with her mommy and daddy.

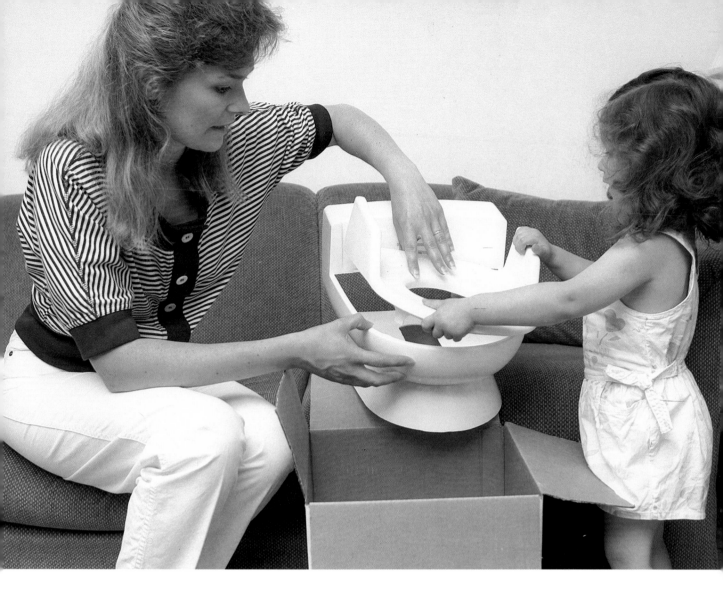

One day, Steffie's mommy brought her a
present. It was a nice new potty. Steffie
liked it right away.

Do you have a potty, too?

Steffie sat on her potty with her clothes on. Steffie's bear, Muffin, sat on it, too.

20

Daddy said, "This little potty is all for you, Steffie. When you are ready, you will urinate and have BMs* in the potty—just the way big people use the big toilet."

*Note to parents: As you read aloud to your child, you may want to substitute the words used in your family for urine and BMs.

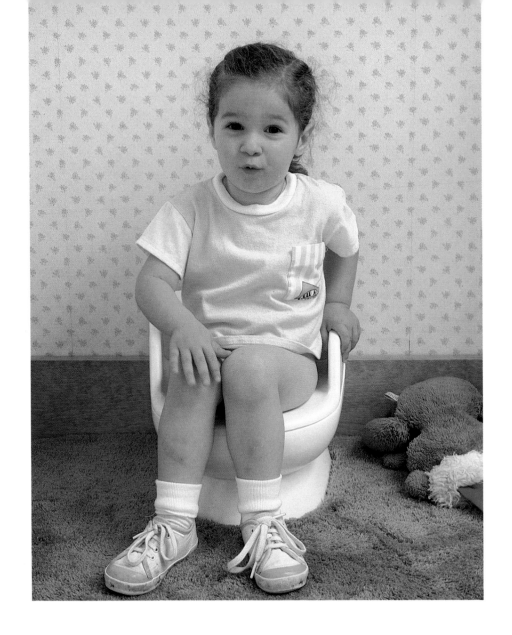

One morning, Steffie tried sitting on
the potty without her diaper. It felt a little cold
at first. But in a minute, it got nice and warm.

Did any urine or BMs go into Steffie's potty? No. Not this time. "That's okay," said Mommy. "Maybe next time."

Steffie sat on her potty every day. One
day she felt urine coming out of her body.
And she heard a little sound. It was the
sound of the urine going into the potty.
Steffie was happy.

Steffie's mommy was happy, too. She smiled and hugged Steffie. Daddy was glad, too.

It is fun to use the potty!

Steffie has a friend named Ben. Ben lives in an apartment building. Ben has a potty, too. He likes to read a book when he sits on his potty. Ben likes his potty.

Steffie always sits down when she goes to the potty. Most of the time, Ben sits down on the potty, too. But sometimes he likes to stand up in front of the toilet.

Boys can stand up when they urinate in the toilet. That is because boys' and girls' bodies are made differently.

Steffie's mommy showed her how to pour the urine into the big toilet. Steffie pressed down the handle and flushed the toilet. Mommy told Steffie that urine and BMs go into pipes under the street.

Ben flushed the toilet at his house, too.
Steffie and Ben waved and said "Bye-bye" to the urine. It was fun!

Some children like to flush. Others do not like it. Do *you* like to flush?

Steffie and Ben both wash their hands
after they use the potty.

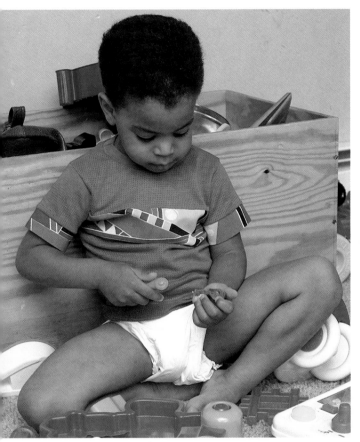
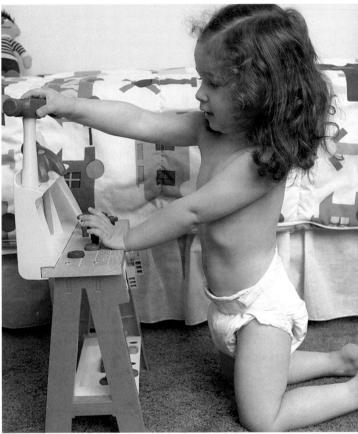

Steffie and Ben like to use the potty. But they still wear diapers most of the time. They are not ready to use the potty *all* of the time.

But one day Steffie said, "I don't want to wear diapers anymore!"

Steffie's mommy said, "Your diaper is dry a lot of the time. You are ready for underpants."

Now Steffie has big-girl pants, just like Mommy. Doesn't she look big?

Ben started wearing underpants, too. He has big-boy pants, just like his daddy.

Ben likes to keep his pants clean and dry. But one day he forgot to use the potty. The pants got wet. The floor got wet, too.

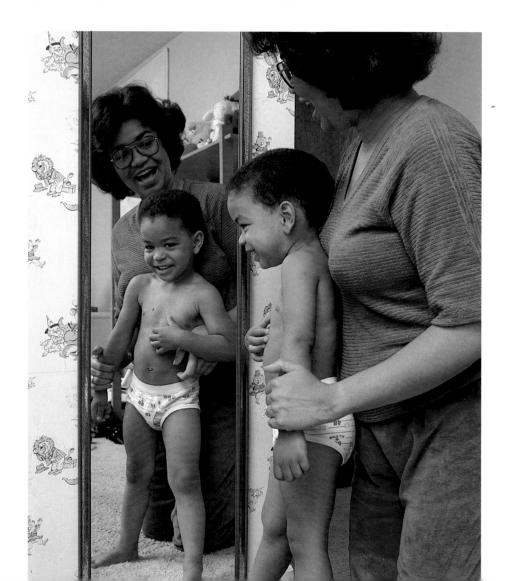

Ben helped mop up. He put the wet
pants in the dirty-clothes basket. He put on
clean pants.

"Don't worry," said Ben's daddy. "All
children have accidents when they are
learning to use the potty."

Sometimes Steffie forgot, too. She
helped clean up.

"Don't be sad," said Steffie's mommy and
daddy. "Next time you will remember to
use the potty."

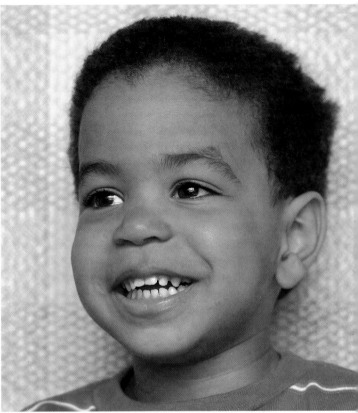

Then Steffie and Ben felt happy again.

When Ben goes to bed, he still wears
a diaper. Ben's mommy says, "In the
morning, you can wear your pants again."

38

Steffie wears a nighttime diaper, too.
Steffie's daddy says, "When you grow
bigger, you will wear pants to bed."

*You* can be like Steffie and Ben. You can
learn to use the potty, too. Then won't you
be proud of yourself!